WHY DOES DADDY SMELL LIKE BBQ?

BY SHANE VIDOVIC

Dedicated to Ashley and Gracyn.
Thank you for tolerating me and all of my wild ideas!!!
I LOVE YOU!!!

Printed in the United States of America

First Printing, November 2020

ISBN 978-0-578-80575-7

Why does Daddy smell like BBQ?

Why does Daddy talk with the butcher for SOOOOO long?

Maybe they tour the world
together in a famous boy band!

Maybe he is a mad scientist that mixes powerful potions in his laboratory!

Why does Daddy chop log
after log?

Maybe he is a lumberjack that can cut down tall trees with one mighty swing of his axe!

Why does Daddy smell like smoke?

Maybe he is a brave knight that has to battle a fire breathing dragon!

Why does Daddy sit by the grill
and wait and wait and wait?

Maybe he is a top-secret agent on a special mission!

Why does Daddy wrap our dinner in aluminum foil?

Maybe he is an elf who wraps
gifts at Santa's secret workshop!

Why does Daddy brush our dinner with BBQ sauce?

Maybe he is a famous artist that
paints pretty portraits!

Why does Daddy cut our dinner so perfectly?

Maybe he is a high-flying ninja that is a master with his sword!

Why does Daddy smell like BBQ?

Because he knows we love it
SOOOOO much!